Skills for Democracy

Promoting Dialogue in Schools

Stephen Preskill
Lois Vermilya
& George Otero

Edited: Justine Moore
Authors: Stephen Preskill, Lois Vermilya & Dr George Otero
Cover Illustration: Hayley Muir
Graphic Layout: Hayley Muir

Published in Australia by:

Hawker Brownlow Education
P.O. Box 580, Cheltenham
Victoria, Australia 3192
Phone: (03) 9555 1344 Fax: (03) 9553 4538
Toll Free Ph: 1800 33 4603 Fax: 1800 15 0445
Website: http://www.hbe.com.au
Email: brown@hbe.com.au

©2000 Hawker Brownlow Education
All Rights Reserved
Printed in Australia

ISBN 1 74025 251 9
CODE #6099

Why is dialogue valuable?

These are challenging times. Rapid and pervasive change dominates our lives. There is an urgent need to reconstruct our leading institutions so as to build a more humane and manageable future. Teaching and learning are two areas where major transitions are needed. Educational success in the new millennium requires more than mastery of academic disciplines. It is not enough for students to know science, history, literature or maths. They must acquire the skills and understandings needed to make democratic deliberation work, not only in the classroom, but in the community at large. Educational practice must be steeped in dialogue to renew learning and teaching and to fulfil the promise of democratic living.

Educational and community leaders are beginning to understand that in order to increase student achievement, communities and their schools must work together differently. Communities are embracing program after program to meet the growing educational, social and health needs of youth and the larger public before, during and after school hours. From full-service schools to after school and early childhood programs, school leaders recognise that meeting the needs of young people requires a much higher level of community and school participation than most models of schooling can accommodate.

New educational initiatives depend upon the ability of everyone involved, especially students, to work together. Building community, identifying concerns and resources, coordinating participation, and planning action together must become habitual practices so that school communities can direct change, not be overwhelmed by it. Success in these community-wide efforts demands frequent public engagement and regular community involvement. Such involvement relies on building trusting, informed, face to face relationships among all those who have a stake in education.

We believe that dialogue will fuel these relationships. Under the right conditions, conversation can (1) generate new knowledge, (2) enhance shared understanding, (3) renew hope, and (4) stimulate collective action. Good dialogue encourages people to solve their problems collaboratively, to see one another as valuable sources of knowledge and experience, and to forge new links with each other. In our view, there is no surer route to community building and to fulfilling the promise of democracy and lifelong learning than through the deepening of good, ongoing dialogue. Such dialogue can increase student achievement, transform teaching and learning and renew relationships that connect communities to their schools. Dialogue, as David Bohm (1996) has pointed out, is a process involving at least two people in which a "stream of meaning" flows among and through the participants. It is a non-competitive process in which "everyone wins". Out of this unobstructed stream of meaning emerges a shared understanding that is new and creative and which has the power to hold people together.

As Benjamin Barber (1984) has noted, public talk is not only a good way to share information, reach new mutual understanding and establish important new community priorities, it is a process that helps us to enhance self-knowledge and build stronger affiliations with others. By deliberating together, we learn more about issues, but we also learn more about each other. Through public discussion, we unveil the variety of defensible viewpoints that are available on almost any subject, and we find out how our neighbours think and feel about these subjects. The more frequently public dialogues are held, the closer people come to a sense of community - that there are certain core values for which we all have high regard and certain core actions to which all are dedicated.

The educational leader Deborah Meier (1995) has said in her book, *The Power of Their Ideas*, that an appropriate metaphor for a good education is a continuing conversation that is just above the heads of the students we teach. It is a conversation that is so compelling, however, that students want to learn all they can so that they can eventually participate too. To play an active role in such a conversation, students must develop the ability to speak articulately and listen respectfully. These are invaluable skills in today's world that can only be honed through ongoing and discerning interactions with others. We believe that involving students in public conversations about controversial issues while they are still in school will not only develop these essential skills but also prepare them to apply these skills as adult citizens.

Dialogue does not only nurture good speakers and listeners, it also produces good critical thinkers. For Meier, effective participation in such a lifelong conversation requires students to learn certain habits of mind that allow them to be thoughtful critics of what others advance. These skills include weighing evidence, taking into account different points of view, and judging the value of new knowledge. The more that students engage in thoughtfully facilitated dialogue, the more they are likely to develop such habits of mind and sharpen their ability to think critically. We often give lip-service to the development of this ability, but schools rarely provide students with opportunities to criticise each other in constructive and mutually enriching ways.

Dialogue is not primarily an individual art; it is a collaborative art. Consequently, it is one of the best ways we know of to engender the skills of cooperation and shared intellectual work. In her now classic article 'Learning in School and Out', developmental psychologist Lauren Resnick criticises schools for ignoring the skills and dispositions that play such a pivotal role in achieving success in the 'real' world of work. Noting that the dominant form of learning in schools is individual, Resnick observes that much activity outside schools is "socially shared". She shows that programs that are most successful in teaching students to think well "are organised around joint accomplishment of tasks, so that elements of the skill take on new meaning in the context of the whole". Nothing is more clearly a shared, joint enterprise than a good discussion about a substantive and disputed issue.

The more students participate in discussions that are engaging and broadly participatory, the more they will learn the value of collaborative work and the more they will learn how to do their part to make the group effective. As Resnick demonstrates so clearly, modern work-places demand such skills and such experience. They are essential to the community as well.

In his book highlighting some of the finest schools in the United States, author George Wood (1992) shows that one of the chief things these schools have in common is a shared commitment to exploring controversial public issues through deliberative dialogue. Among the skills these dialogues teach is effective use of the spoken word, accessing information from a variety of perspectives, listening and responding in the full meaning of what is heard, criticising other people's views closely and constructively, and using expert opinion wisely without becoming subservient to it. We believe that the only way these skills can be learnt is for students to engage regularly in thoughtfully planned and skillfully facilitated dialogues. Teachers must provide plenty of opportunities for students to speak to each other, to challenge one another, and to reach new understandings together.

Skills for Democracy School Dialogue Project

With the support of the New Mexico Dispute Resolution Centre, we invited some middle and high school teachers to join us in two days of deliberation and activity about principles and practices of conducting good dialogues. The facilitators of these workshops introduced many useful ideas to the participants, but the participants themselves were also energetic contributors and actively shared many of their experiences of leading young people in dialogue. In thinking about the issues and concerns that are most important in making discussion of controversial issues work, we have concluded that there are six key questions about which all participants should be aware. They are:

1. Why is dialogue valuable? (A question we have attempted to answer in this section.)
2. What are some of the conditions for good dialogue?
3. What are some good ways to get dialogue started?
4. What are some good ways to keep dialogue going?
5. How can we deepen dialogue?
6. How can we connect dialogue to action?

What are some of the conditions for good dialogue?

One set of conditions has to do with the attitudes or dispositions that participants should practise to create good dialogue. When we lead discussions, we try to get participants to be aware of these dispositions. We also model them and encourage participants to adopt these dispositions themselves. We can never expect more than partial success in acting on these dispositions, but even naming them and being aware of them helps participants to move toward more collaborative and respectful interactions. We have found the following to be especially relevant and useful:

1. Hospitality
2. Participation
3. Mindfulness
4. Humility
5. Mutuality
6. Deliberation
7. Appreciation
8. Hope
9. Autonomy

Hospitality

By hospitality we mean the sort of inviting, welcoming, engaging spirit that prevails in dialogue sessions where each person feels that his or her involvement is essential. Hospitality communicates to each participant, 'without you we are diminished; we are incomplete'. It also suggests that dialogue is an occasion for celebration and for acknowledging the power and potential of collective talk and action. Additionally, hospitality implies that participants are attentive to the physical setting, to seating arrangements that encourage engagement, and to helping one another become comfortable together.

Participation

Although no one who joins a public gathering to discuss controversial issues should feel compelled to talk, the disposition of participation reinforces the notion that there are many ways to contribute and that each type of contribution has an impact on group deliberations. Participation also implies that there should be a way, however subtle, for the group to acknowledge each person's influence.

Mindfulness

Discussion cannot be as effective without individual and group mindfulness. It means paying attention at many different levels. We need to be mindful of what each person says, how it is said, and how it relates to what has already been said. But we also must be mindful of what is not being said, of issues that are being avoided, and of participants who are feeling silenced. Finally, we must pay attention to the arc of the entire discussion and note how well it is addressing the issues that the group has gathered to explore.

Humility

This well-known disposition is a reminder that no one person's knowledge and understanding are total. When humility is practised, participants accept that there is always more to learn and that the group's collective wisdom benefits each individual. Humility motivates us to gather with others to learn from them and to re-experience the pleasure of moving from ignorance to knowledge, from not-knowing to greater understanding. Humility also demands deep listening. In the best discussions, humble participants listen at three levels - they listen to self, they listen to others, and they listen for the shared meaning.

Mutuality

This disposition suggests that the more each participant is free to contribute what she or he knows, the more everyone else profits. Mutuality says that when I allow other people the space to speak, when I give others the room to share their experience, I am also advantaged because I also expand my experiential horizons and deepen my understanding. Mutuality also implies a collective commitment to inquiry, to raising questions to foster both individual and collective understanding.

Deliberation

This notion goes to the heart of good dialogue. It refers to the willingness of participants to explore issues as fully as possible by offering arguments and counter-arguments supported by evidence, data and logic. Deliberation obliges us to take strong, well substantiated stands unless there are good reasons not to do so. When we embrace deliberation, the reasons we offer for the positions we take are primary. However, deliberation also requires us to remain alert to the reasons other participants put forward and to adopt them if they are sufficiently compelling and persuasive.

Appreciation

This is one of the most neglected of dispositions. It calls on us to take the time to acknowledge a useful insight or an illuminating contribution. It implies that the opportunity to discuss difficult issues with others is wonderful and life-enhancing and that we should seize every chance to express our gratitude to others. It is part of the celebratory aspect of public discussion mentioned in the discussion of hospitality.

Hope

In his *Pedagogy of Hope*, the late Paulo Freire (1994) mentions that he cannot comprehend human existence or the struggle to improve it without a foundation in hope. As difficult as reform and social change can be, hope must be one of the mainstays of good dialogue. Hope assumes that a great deal of good can emerge from people taking the time to gather together to talk about the important issues of the day. Most of all, hope affirms our collective capacity to use dialogue to envision new possibilities and to act on behalf of the common good.

Autonomy

This disposition reminds us of the responsibility to stand up for what we believe. It does not negate in any way the value of learning from the group or from sometimes adopting the views of the group. It simply says that there are times when we must defy the collective deliberations of the group and go our own way, however contrary that may appear to others. It reinforces the idea that groups are strongest when the identities of individual members are given their due and when each person's passions and commitments are allowed a fair hearing.[1]

---

[1] For more detail on these dispositions, see Stephen Brookfield and Stephen Preskill, *Discussion as a Way of Teaching*, Jossey-Bass, (1999).

The teachers with whom we met to discuss the dialogue process identified many additional conditions that they suggested may be necessary to move discussion in fruitful and mutually satisfying directions. Among the conditions that they noted:

1. Establishing a process to ensure that careful listening takes place
2. Maintaining a safe, comfortable environment
3. Having expressed feelings accepted without judgment
4. Being flexible enough to generate new concepts and consider new possibilities
5. Creating an atmosphere in which participants are absolutely honest with each other
6. Keeping the size of the group small enough for good interaction
7. Showing respect toward all participants
8. Keeping the discussion topic relevant and interesting for all participants
9. Making sure to take turns - avoid speaking too much or too little
10. Including a skillful and sensitive facilitator
11. Keeping the discussion questions open-ended and spontaneous
12. Maintaining passion and excitement as participants exchange ideas
13. Airing differences honestly
14. Remembering to affirm others within the group
15. Talking about issues over which there are genuine differences and divergent experiences
16. Remaining tolerant toward others and striving to understand their opinions, their experiences
17. Encouraging contribution from many participants
18. Avoiding a situation in which participants are coerced to contribute
19. Establishing conditions so that participants have relatively equal levels of knowledge and information
20. Omitting personal agendas, participating for the sake of group growth and group understanding
21. Avoiding personal vendettas
22. Keeping the energy and enthusiasm high
23. Participating not to win but to enhance understanding
24. Creating an environment in which many right answers are possible
25. Participating by listening more than speaking

The teachers with whom we worked also suggested some activities that they have found conducive to creating a good atmosphere for dialogue. These activities seem to share a few key characteristics - that students need to get to know one another before they can engage in productive talk and that they need to establish some basic level of trust with one another. A few of the proposed activities follow:

1. Students create and display pictorial autobiographies centred on their nicknames.

2. Nonverbal getting acquainted. Pairs of students tell each other about themselves nonverbally, essentially introducing each other through charades. After giving each other information about themselves nonverbally, each student introduces the other student to the class, but this time with words.

3. Group Collages. Give groups of students a theme with which to build a group collage. Have them brainstorm all the group's associations with the theme and then select a lot of magazine pictures to illustrate the theme. Have them present the final product to the class. Sample themes: Faces of all Races. Sports of all Sorts. Generation Gap. Life in the 21st century.

In the spirit of dialogue, we invite you to participate in a 'conversation' with the authors by offering some of your own conditions for dialogue and your own activities for establishing healthy conditions. What are five to ten conditions that you regard as particularly important and that have been especially valuable to you in setting the stage for engaging discussion? What are two or three activities that are likely to produce these desired conditions?

Conditions

1.

2.

3.

4.

5.

Activities

1.

2.

3.

Temperature Reading

Time: Anywhere from 10 minutes to a full class session

Materials: None, except a list of the categories

Objective: To get people talking authentically about their experience in a group setting

Procedures:

1. Tell students that you want to take a temperature reading, not of the outside, but of the inside of each person in the class. Share the purpose in writing or verbally.

   The purpose of a temperature check is to give every participant time and opportunity to say what is on his or her mind or in his or her heart.

2. Mention that there are five categories to consider speaking to, yet students should, over time, feel free to say what needs to be said.

   The categories are: *Appreciations, New Information, Puzzlements, Concerns with Recommendations,* and *Hopes.*

   Appreciations is the category to use when expressing how much you learnt from Jane's presentation or how grateful you are to Keith for sharing his personal experience or how much you enjoyed last evening's dinner. The *New Information* category permits announcements, the sharing of the day's agenda or changes in scheduling, the time for the next exam or the due date for an upcoming essay. *Puzzlements* are questions you have for which you don't necessarily expect an answer. These might include a comment from yesterday that you didn't quite understand, lack of clarity about the purposes of an assignment, or general perplexity about the meaning of life. The *Concerns with Recommendations* category permits people to raise a concern or voice an objection to something. In order to keep things constructive, any concern that is voiced must be accompanied by a suggestion as to how to remedy the problem, though no one is obligated to adopt the suggestion. The person raising the concern must have given some thought not only to the problem but also to how it can be addressed. Finally, there is the *Hopes* category. Relevant to this category are: hopes or expectations for the day, hopes or aspirations for the semester, things that you hope won't happen.

3. In our experience, students feel uncomfortable with the temperature check when it is first introduced. Yet, we can't think of a better way to begin to cultivate the conditions that will support rich dialogue within the classroom. Frequently, the first day it is used, few people will speak and then only briefly. Usually, by the second day, and almost invariably by the third, most people are beginning to get the feel of it and enjoy the relatively unstructured discussions. Should the discussion begin to degenerate, you can remind the group of the categories.

4. The temperature check format is often so successful that lengthy and exciting discussions are generated, though it is usually a good idea to impose time limits. But if the discussion is going well as the time limit approaches, you might want to mention it and ask if the group would like to continue the temperature check or move on.

Good Ways to Get Dialogue Started

How the discussion begins can sometimes set the tone for how productively participants interact and exchange ideas with one another throughout the rest of the conversation. There are many ways to initiate discussion but perhaps the most important thing is to stimulate thought and to trigger a reaction without imposing a particular point of view or limiting opportunities for individual expression. Choosing the right question or the right activity has to do with opening up the range of possible directions or responses, not closing them down.

Before doing anything, though, it is a good idea to establish a space for dialogue by forming the chairs into a circle, actively welcoming participants, and celebrating the opportunity that this gathering signifies. Participants need to know from the beginning that their involvement is important. The circle underscores the fact that every individual should be visible to all others and that each person's contribution is invited. By celebrating the occasion of dialogue, participants get the sense from the beginning that this assemblage of people is significant and that wonderful, unexpected things can happen when they start talking to each other.

It is also useful, before the discussion begins, to help participants understand that real dialogue is a collaborative, non-competitive activity in which people seek both increased understanding and common ground. Dialogue embraces complexity and flexibility and strives to find room for many points of view. Dialogue should be contrasted with debate. Debate tends to be contentious and puts a high premium on prevailing over one's opponent. Below is a comparison of dialogue and debate that may be useful to share with people as they begin the hard work of collaborating together in discussion.

Comparison of Dialogue and Debate

Adapted from 'Comparison of Dialogue and Debate' by Sheldon Barnes and the Boston Area Educators for Social Responsibility Dialogue Group, 1983

Dialogue is talking with others.	Debate is talking at others.
Dialogue is collaborative: two or more sides working together toward common understanding.	Debate is oppositional: two sides oppose each other and attempt to prove each other wrong.
In dialogue, one listens to the other side(s) in order to understand, find meaning and reach agreement.	In debate, one listens to the other side in order to find flaws and disagreement.

Dialogue enlarges and possibly changes a participant's point of view.	Debate affirms a participant's own point of view.
Dialogue complicates positions and issues.	Debate simplifies positions and issues.
Dialogue is flexible in nature.	Debate is rigid in nature.
Dialogue stresses the skill of synthesis.	Debate stresses the skill of analysis.
Dialogue strives for multiplicity in perspective.	Debate strives for singularity in perspective.
Dialogue calls for temporarily suspending one's beliefs.	Debate calls for investing wholeheartedly in one's beliefs.
In dialogue, everyone is part of the problem.	In debate, one person, solution or viewpoint wins over the other.
Dialogue affirms the idea of people learning from each other.	Debate affirms the idea of people individually in competition with each other.
Dialogue remains open-minded.	Debate insists on a final answer.

Once people have a clear understanding of what it means to engage in an authentic dialogue, a simple way to get things started - that allows everyone to put forward a view - is to ask what issue or problem has been bothering them lately. Participants are invited to talk briefly about this issue, but they are also encouraged to listen for patterns or recurring themes that may emerge as the discussion proceeds. These themes or patterns can then be used as a basis for future discussions which will have relevance and value for all of the discussants. Along the same lines, discussion can begin by having participants generate questions for which they do not have answers and by which they are genuinely puzzled. These questions can then form the foundation for subsequent exchanges. Sentence completion exercises are another way to get things going. Participants are invited to complete sentences like 'The thing that really made me angry when I read the newspaper today was…' The discussion that ensues when small groups share their completions can be eye-opening and stimulating and generate much more discussion about how the group feels about leading controversial issues.

Another way to get discussion started, especially when the participants do not know each other, is to distribute a controversial quotation to the group and invite their reaction. A favourite one about the educational system is simply: 'Schools never take the lead on social change; they merely reproduce the inequalities that already exist in the larger society'. If there are teachers in the group, they will feel compelled to disagree strongly. Others, such as parents, will also be inclined to take a strong stand against this claim. However, there should enough people in the group to argue in favour of the position. Invariably, this quote - and ones like it - get people excited and stimulated, which leads to some energetic and passionate exchanges.

When fairly large groups of people come together, it is sometimes difficult to make people comfortable enough to interact productively. One way around this is a technique called *Snowballing* or *Pyramid*. In this process, a topic of mutual interest to the group is chosen and participants jot down their initial thoughts on the question. Each participant is then asked to join with one other person to discuss their initial reactions to the issue. After perhaps ten minutes of chatting and sharing, each pair joins another pair to form quartets. The groups of four then spend another ten minutes or so sharing their initial answers and building on what was discussed in the pairs. When time is up, each group of four joins another quartet to create octets or groups of eight. The process continues in this way until the whole group is reunited. *Snowballing* combines the intimacy of small group pairings with the breadth and scope of large group discussion, because over time both kinds of groupings are encouraged. It is also a way for people in large groups to get to know one another more gradually than is possible in a single large group.

Sometimes what is needed to get people talking is just to provide a space for each person to speak in turn. This is what the *Circle of Voices* process is all about. With *Circle of Voices*, participants are invited to form their chairs into a circle and to respond to a question or simply to share something about themselves. One person begins and speaks without interruption for no more than two minutes. The person to the first speaker's left then has an opportunity to say something, again limited to two minutes. The opportunity to speak makes its way around the circle. Once everyone has had a chance to speak, general discussion may begin. This process loosens people up, affords them an opportunity to speak without the threat of interruption or challenge, and can reveal a great deal about the people gathered in the circle. It helps participants to get to know one another, but it also allows each person to set the terms and limits on how much is disclosed.

Sentence Completion

Time: 30 minutes

Materials: Handouts with sentences to be filled in

Objective: To get people talking to each other about something controversial

Procedures:

1. Group people in a circle and distribute to them incomplete sentences that include a blank space. Examples are: The thing that made me really angry when I read the newspaper this morning was: _____.
Or It was really affirming when you mentioned _____.
Or The question that keeps coming up for me but for which I don't have a good answer is _____.

2. Next ask them to complete the sentence that you have distributed. Have them do this individually.

3. When participants have completed their sentences, have them share what they have written with three other people. Allow discussion in these small groups to ensue.

4. Have the members of the small group choose one participant's sentence completion that they feel is especially intriguing or provocative.

5. Bring each group's chosen sentence completion back to the large group for general discussion.

Memorable Quotes

Time: 30 minutes

Materials: Whatever the group is reading at the time

Objective: To get people talking about something controversial

Procedures:

1. Ask participants to bring current reading materials with them to the discussion group.

2. Invite them to identify a quotation from the reading that they find interesting, memorable, insulting or puzzling.

3. Share these quotations in small groups of four participants each.

4. Identify one quote from the small group discussion that seems especially rich for further discussion and bring it back to the large group.

5. Have each group introduce into general discussion the quotation chosen and use it to raise questions and to make connections among the different quotes.

Snowballing

Time: Varies depending on size of group - about an hour

Materials: None

Objective: To get people talking in small, intimate groups, as well as in increasingly larger groups

Procedures:

1. Ask a question about a topic of mutual interest and ask everyone to write down their responses individually. Give them about five minutes.

2. Invite participants to pair up with another person and share with each other what they have written. Allow another ten minutes.

3. Now have participants form quartets to share their responses and to continue the discussion. Allow another 15 minutes.

4. Ask participants once again to double the size of their groups - now to groups of eight or octets.

5. Continue in this way until the entire group is reunited. Finish the discussion in the group as a whole and reflect on the process of *Snowballing*.

Circle of Voices[2]

Time: Varies depending on the size of the group

Materials: None

Objective: To let everyone speak in a safe, conflict-free environment
                To let everyone hear the rich diversity in the group

Procedures:

1. Arrange the chairs in a circle so that everyone has a clear view of everyone else.

2. Choose a topic upon which everyone can comfortably comment and give each participant an opportunity to speak without interruption for no more than two minutes.

3. Move around the circle left to right in order. Do not comment on what anyone has said while she or he is speaking or afterwards until everyone has had a chance to speak. You may take notes if you wish as each person contributes, but put special effort into listening attentively to what each person has to say.

4. After everyone has spoken, participants are free to comment on what different individuals said or to make a contribution about the value of the *Circle of Voices* process.

[2]Adapted from activities through the Study Circles Resource Center, P.O. Box 203, 697 Pomfret Street, Pomfret, CN 06258 USA

The teachers we worked with also suggested some additional activities to get dialogue started. A few of these are listed below.

1. The teacher provides each student with a definition and/or origin of his or her first name. During the next couple of class sessions, students draw a picture that represents the meaning or derivation of their name. They also interview their parents to determine how they came to acquire their name. In the end, drawings are displayed and students give brief presentations about their names. This entire process works to help students get to know each other and to learn to talk about themselves in public.

2. Last names. Have the students share the background of their last names. This is a chance to document diversity and acknowledge our ancestors.

3. Personal collages in class. Mix painting and collage as a form. Have the students produce a work that has personal meaning for them and that they can share with the rest of the class.

Perhaps you have some additional thoughts about how to get discussion started. Feel free to list a few of your ideas here.

1.

2.

3.

What are some good ways to keep dialogue going?

Sometimes, despite our best efforts, discussions that start out well seem to go nowhere. There are many explanations for this. In some cases, one or two people dominate the exchange; in other cases, too much agreement saps the conversation of its energy. In still other situations, the pace of the discussion is too slow, or the process for exploring the topic at hand is not sufficiently varied. Perhaps most common of all is the tendency for individuals to speak without connecting their observations to those of others; that is, to neglect the value and power of conversational collaboration and continuity. Of course, this isn't just the responsibility of individual participants; it is a goal that good facilitators must also pursue. How discussion leaders and other participants ask questions of one another, how they listen to each other, and how they respond to one another can sometimes make the difference between a perfunctory exercise and a really exciting exchange of ideas.

It is our contention, therefore, that discussions are most likely to persist when participants are acutely conscious of what has been said and are eager to relate their own comments to what others have contributed. Furthermore, we suggest that when people listen carefully, pose questions inquisitively, and respond to others sensitively, good discussion can be sustained indefinitely.

Asking good questions that encourage participants to probe more deeply or to elaborate more fully is one simple way to keep the conversation going. Questions that ask for more information are one way to do this. For example:

> 'What else can you add to what you've already said?'
> 'How do you know that?'
> 'What evidence can you offer to support you claim?'
> 'What else follows from what you've said so far?'

Questions that seek clarification are a good way to encourage more precise and careful thinking and to help everyone make sense of the group's deliberations. Examples include:

> 'Can you give an example of what you mean?'
> 'Can you put that another way or can you offer an analogy that might help us understand?'
> 'How is that different from what we've already heard?'

Perhaps most useful of all are questions that link and extend the discussion, that promote the collaboration and continuity we referred to earlier. Possible examples are:

'Is that similar to what Raymond just said?'
'How does your comment relate to the three previous ones?'
'What themes have emerged in our discussion so far and what else do we need to know about this?'

Participants and facilitators alike should practise asking different kinds of questions in discussion. In fact, it is useful at times to stop being a provider of information altogether. For a while try being just a questioner. What are you seeing that you didn't see before?

Another way to foster collaboration and continuity is to address it head-on through something like the *Circular Response* exercise. In this process, participants gather in a circle so that everyone has a clear view of everyone else. Each person is instructed that she or he has three minutes to speak without interruption from anyone else in the group. So far it is similar to the *Circle of Voices* process, but there is one additional requirement that makes it quite different. With the exception of the first speaker, each person in the circle must begin his or her remarks by summarising the comments of the previous speaker, referring to the tone of what was said, and then checking with that previous speaker to make sure that the present speaker has captured these remarks accurately. Only then may the present speaker initiate her own comments and they should spring from and be connected to the previous speaker's contribution. The opportunity to speak makes its way around the circle until everyone has spoken. When the circle is complete, general discussion may ensue. What makes this exercise unique is the object of building continuity through careful listening. It reminds participants that the point of discussion is to collaboratively deliberate, not simply to get something off one's chest, and that each comment that is made should relate to what has already been stated. This can be a difficult and frustrating exercise, but it is usually worthwhile because it fosters dispositions that go to the heart of effective group dialogue.

Another way to focus on the practice of good listening is by pairing people and giving them opportunities to alternate between being a speaker and a listener. The speaker's job is easy. He has to talk for about five minutes on some preselected topic. The listener's work is much more difficult and is a reminder, in itself, that listening is the most challenging part of good discussion. The listener must be able to demonstrate in a variety of ways that she is listening closely and really cares about what is being said. Some of the ways in which this can be done are to:

❖ Maintain good eye contact.

❖ Use body language that is directed toward the speaker.

❖ Interject with verbal cues that show the speaker is being followed.

❖ Paraphrase what is being said occasionally.

❖ Pose an occasional question where appropriate and needed.

❖ In general, exert effort to show that as listener you are devoting all of your energy to listening.

There is a rather enjoyable way in a group to practise good questioning, good listening and good responding. We call it the *Conversational Moves* activity. (For more on this activity and others like, it see Stephen Brookfield and Stephen Preskill, *Discussion as a Way of Teaching*, Jossey-Bass, 1999.) In this exercise, each participant receives an index card that has one of the following conversational moves listed on it (see below). The person who holds a card with a particular move on it must practise that move at least once during the discussion. When the discussion is over, the discussion leader should share all of the moves with the group and point out that virtually all of them are designed to strengthen connections among group members and to reinforce the notion that discussion is a collaborative process. Here is a list (hardly exhaustive) of some possible *conversational moves*:[3]

Ask a question or make a comment that shows you are interested in what another person has said.

Ask a question or make a comment that encourages someone else to elaborate on something that a person has said.

Make a comment that underscores the link between two people's contributions. Make this link explicit in your comment.

Use body language (in a slightly exaggerated way) to show interest in what different speakers are saying.

Make a comment indicating that you found another person's ideas useful or helpful. Be specific as to why this was the case.

Contribute something that builds on or springs from what someone has said. Be explicit about the way you are building on the other person's thoughts.

---

[3] op. cit., pp.101-102

Make a comment that at least partly paraphrases a point someone has already made.

Make a summary observation that takes into account several people's contributions and that touches on a recurring theme in the discussion.

At an appropriate moment, ask the group for a minute's silence to slow the pace of conversation and give you and others time to think.

Find a way to express appreciation for the enlightenment you have gained from the discussion. Try to be specific about what it was that helped you understand something better.

Disagree with someone in a respectful and constructive way.

There are, of course, many other *conversational moves* that could be assigned, and, in fact, it might be interesting for the group at some point to devise their own *conversational moves*. The point is, however, that there are many things *all* participants in a discussion can do to build continuity, foster collaboration, and make it a truly cooperative enterprise. These are all things we can do to keep discussion moving in fresh and stimulating new directions.

Take a few moments to list some additional ideas on how to keep discussion going in interesting and fruitful directions.

1.

2.

3.

Circular Response

Time: Depends on the size of the group

Materials: None

Objectives: To enhance listening and to build continuity in discussion

Procedures:

1. Gather in a circle just as in circle of voices and explain to everyone that they have no more than three minutes to speak and that they may speak during this time without interruption.

2. However, unlike *Circle of Voices*, they must begin their comments (with the sole exception of the first speaker) by summarising the comments of the previous speaker. They also must receive some sort of affirmation from the previous speaker that their summary accurately reflects what the last speaker said.

3. Each speaker then may proceed by making additional comments that in some way spring from what was previously said.

4. The discussion continues around the circle with each new speaker summarising the contribution of the previous participant, checking with the previous speaker for accuracy, and then extending the conversation by building on what the previous speaker stated.

5. The process continues until everyone has had a chance to speak. Only after everyone has spoken may general, unrestricted discussion begin.

The current debate over mandatory sentencing provides a simple example of an issue that can be used to practise *Circular Response*.

Mandatory Sentencing - Five Choices

Here is a range of possible positions on society's use of mandatory sentencing:

Position 1
Mandatory sentencing should be abolished because it is cruel and inflexible.

Position 2
Mandatory sentencing should be abolished because it is unjustly applied.

Position 3
Mandatory sentencing should be retained because justice requires it.

Position 4
Mandatory sentencing should be retained and made easier to implement because it serves a useful purpose.

Position 5
Madatory sentencing should be abolished because imprisoning young people for relatively minor offences can turn them into hardened criminals.

Expose the students to these different positions and give them a chance to think about and respond to each of them. Let them consider which of these positions they find most defensible, but also give them an opportunity to generate an entirely new position of their own. As the students deliberate about the strengths and weaknesses of these different positions and explore new options, have them also consider these questions:

Which position is most likely to promote principles of justice?

Which position best serves the interests of society?

Which position is most likely to lead to a safe and secure community?

Overall, which is the position you are inclined to support?

Paired Listening

Time: About 15 minutes

Materials: None

Objective: To practise listening skills

Procedures:

1. Pair up with another person. Designate one person the speaker and the other person the listener. Do this for five minutes and then switch roles.

2. The speaker may talk about anything (usually something autobiographical), but the focus is on the listener.

3. How many ways can the listener show that she or he is really listening and really cares about what is being said?

4. Some signs of good listening are:

   ❖ maintaining eye contact
   ❖ directing supportive body language toward the speaker
   ❖ nodding, smiling (where appropriate)
   ❖ maintaining sober but sympathetic demeanour (where appropriate)
   ❖ interjecting with various sounds to denote that the speaker's meaning is being followed
   ❖ paraphrasing occasionally what is being heard
   ❖ questioning occasionally for clarification
   ❖ exerting real effort in general to hear what is being said accurately.

5. Ask the listener to make use of as many of the above as possible.

6. Reflect on the experience of being in the *Paired Listening* exercise.

Conversational Moves

Time: About 45 minutes

Materials: A series of cards, each of which represents a different conversational move

Goal: To role-play the rich diversity of ways in which discussants can contribute to and enhance conversation

Procedures:

1. Distribute to each participant one of the following instructions:

   ❖ Ask a question that shows you are interested in what another participant said.
   ❖ Ask a question or make a comment that encourages someone else to build on or elaborate on what someone else has said.
   ❖ Make a comment that underscores the link between two people's contributions.
   ❖ Use body language to show interest in what different speakers are saying.
   ❖ Make a comment showing that you found another person's ideas useful or helpful.
   ❖ Contribute something that builds on or springs from what someone else has said.
   ❖ Make a comment that paraphrases another person's comments.
   ❖ Summarise the discussion so far.
   ❖ Ask for a moment of silence to slow the pace of conversation and to give others time to think about what has been said.
   ❖ Find a way to express appreciation for how the group has helped you understand an issue better.
   ❖ Disagree with someone in a respectful and constructive way.

2. Begin the discussion about a mutually interesting topic and make sure that you do what the card instructs at least once during the discussion.

3. At the end of the discussion, distribute all of the instructions to everyone so that they can see the many ways in which they can contribute to discussion.

4. Invite the group to comment on these different roles and to add to the possible roles that different discussants can play.

What are some good ways to deepen dialogue?

Discussion can be like a journey. It takes a great deal of preparation to begin and a lot of gumption to keep going. But once you are underway, your momentum often carries you along. More important, as you set out into uncharted territory, the opportunities for new adventure and new discoveries also increase. It is during these times that the real benefits of the journey begin to accrue; the goals that spurred the expedition in the first place draw near. When we deepen the dialogue, we take the leap toward unexpected insights, startling findings, transformational learning. When we deepen the dialogue, our previous struggles to understand one another begin to bear fruit.

Deepening the dialogue has many implications. It means that participants are listening more attentively and probing for new understanding more effectively. It means that participants are disclosing their feelings more honestly and revealing their viewpoints more frankly. It also means that participants are attempting to take multiple perspectives into account and are able to derive value from a variety of points of view. Finally, it means that discussion has continuity, that it is building on the contributions of each participant to create a relatively cohesive and cumulative whole. In other words, the progress that is being made individually and collectively to increase understanding would not have been possible without the involvement of all the discussants present.

As we deepen the dialogue, the techniques we have used to begin and sustain discussion remain important, but they also fade into the background somewhat as we learn to experience the evolving, organic, life-of-its-own quality of an authentic exchange of ideas. Dialogue at its best and at its deepest transforms power relationships, allowing all participants to be both learners and teachers and bringing everyone to the conviction that no single person has the full answer. Although the full answer always eludes us, even our partial, tentative conclusions invariably result from considering the many points of view that are represented in every group. As the dialogue deepens, we continue to take strong, individual stands on the issues discussed, but the investment of ego in the discussion's outcome also lessens significantly. Our concern is with the dialogue itself, whether important issues are stated, whether everyone has the opportunity to contribute something valuable, whether the desire to inquire further and to advocate strongly is respected and nurtured. As important as our own views are, we willingly suspend judgment about the outcome and put the group's continuing and constructive deliberations at the centre of our concerns.

The teacher has a special role to play in facilitating the deepening of dialogue. It is not enough for the teacher just to be proficient in guiding the exchange of ideas; she or he must assume a leadership role in transforming the way participants interact with each other. A lesson plan, no matter how comprehensive, cannot capture this special role. This means that the teacher consciously takes the lead in changing power relationships and reinforces the idea that dialogue is a way of more authentically being together, as well as an opportunity to learn from each other. The teacher also actively strives to create a community of learners in which no participant's self-interest interferes with the common good. As the dialogue deepens, the teacher helps the participants to see that it is the conversation itself that leads - not one participant, not even the teacher. Words cannot fully capture the feelings we experience and the wisdom we gain from dialogue in which each person gives up a little part of himself for the sake of group growth. Achieving this is the discussion leader's greatest challenge and the source of her greatest satisfaction.

Perhaps at the heart of deepening the dialogue is the practice of deep listening. Deep listening entails three carefully cultivated habits - listening to self, listening to others and listening to the emerging shared meaning.

By listening to self we mean being attentive to one's own assumptions, beliefs and feelings and how they shape one's opinions. Listening to self calls on discussion participants to heighten their consciousness about the roots of their viewpoints, to identify prejudices and biases, and to be aware of internal contradictions. Listening to self calls on discussants to come to terms with who they are, to confront their individual identities, and to make this growing self-knowledge an important part of constructive but challenging conversation.

By listening to others we mean bending over backwards to understand what the rest of the group is trying to communicate. Who really are the people we have joined in discussion? What experiences have influenced their opinions? What beliefs and assumptions underlie their contributions to the group's deliberations? Even when I disagree, how can I show others that I understand what they are saying and that I respect and appreciate their comments? In what ways are they contributing to the shared understanding and meaning that is being constructed by the group as a whole?

Finally, by listening for the shared meaning we focus on attending to the whole. The emphasis here is not primarily on what each participant has offered individually but on what has been fashioned out of these individual contributions. Once a building is erected, the materials that went into it are relatively unimportant; it is the value and meaning of the final structure that ultimately matters. The same is true when discussion deepens. What are the overall understandings and feelings that emerge once the discussion comes to a close? What do we take away from the experience that cannot be reduced to any one idea or comment? It is when participants begin to view dialogue in this way that we know the discussion is deepening, that it is moving from the specific to the general, from isolated, individual experiences to co-created meaning and value.

We have included some techniques and activities for deepening dialogue. One highly successful and widely used process is the *National Issues Forum*. Using this process, discussion participants consider three or four well-grounded alternative approaches to a controversial issue and, by the conclusion of the dialogue, are asked to choose the approach that they believe is most likely to be successful in addressing the problem. This process deepens dialogue by exposing participants to some carefully thought out solutions to a difficult problem and giving them the opportunity to exchange views about the strengths and weaknesses of each solution. This process moves the discussion away from personal agendas and encourages people to critique approaches that enjoy broad support.

Another process that also deepens discussion in a completely different manner is *Multiple Perspectives*. Here the group continues a discussion - perhaps begun under the *National Issues Forum* guidelines - but now identifies all the stakeholders that they think should have an important voice in shaping policy around the issue. Once these stakeholders are identified, each member of a small group is asked to role-play that stakeholder, making an effort to speak from that person's perspective. For instance, if a member of a small group is assigned the role of parent, that discussant must comment on the issue as a parent would with the interests of a parent in mind. In this exercise there are opportunities to assume the roles of many different stakeholders, and through this process to experience the wide range of views and the many competing social interests that emerge on most controversial issues.

Still another technique is *listening with the third, fourth and fifth ear*, or as we have already indicated, listening to self, listening to others and listening for shared meaning. In this simple exercise, participants are encouraged to listen intensively at many different levels, but are aided in doing so by wearing blindfolds. The use of blindfolds eliminates reliance on visual cues and forces participants to rely almost entirely on the power of close, wide-awake listening in making the discussion work.

Below are a couple of additional ideas that teachers have suggested for deepening discussion:

1. **Validate and Defend**
   As an alternative to relying on teacher approval, have students validate and defend to the teacher another student's comment or viewpoint. Student love to advocate for their peers, and such processes build trust and generate a stronger sense of shared meaning.

2. **Fear in the Hat**
   Have students write down a fear. Put the fears in a hat and pull them out one by one anonymously, giving students an opportunity to give advice on how to handle the fear. This exercise also builds trust and gives students a strengthened sense of community.

There are many ways to build and deepen communication skills. Two well-known techniques are *I Messages* and *Speaking from Feeling*. For information on these techniques and similar ones see these publications by the Dispute Resolution Center:

What are some ideas that you suggest to deepen dialogue?

1.

2.

3.

Issues Forum

Time: At least one hour (could be extended for greater depth)
Plus: one week of concentrated research to prepare study materials for alternative solutions
NOTE: Prepared study booklets are also available to schools and other groups through:
National Issues Forum
100 Commons Road
Dayton, Ohio 45459-2777 USA

Materials: Researched materials that provide three or four alternative solutions to selected controversial issue

Objective: To hold a discussion about a vital public issue in which participants are encouraged to weigh the strengths and weaknesses of three or four alternative solutions and to reach at least a tentative but reasoned conclusion about the alternative preferred

Procedures:

1. Conduct research to outline key data and points of view for three or four alternative solutions to a controversial issue.

5. Written Materials Outline:

    What's the problem? - problem viewpoint
    What should be done? - proposed solution
    Why this course of action? - key arguments in favour
    What do critics say? - key arguments against

6. Distribute study materials to be read before discussion.

7. Poll the group as to their opinions on the controversial issue.

8. Present the group with three or four alternative solutions to the problem and get their reactions.

9. Give the group enough time to compare and contrast alternatives, 'to try them on for size'.

10. Invite the group to offer their tentative conclusions about the solution they find most satisfactory.

11. Poll the group again as to their current opinions on the same controversial issue.

Multiple Perspectives[4]

Time: One hour (can be extended to two hours for more depth)

Materials: Two large pieces of posterboard cut into two circles. One large piece and one slightly smaller piece, pinned together at centre with wing fastener, divided into six to eight sections ('pie pieces'). Also post-it notes.

Objective: To practise how to explore a controversial issue from the multiple perspectives of different stakeholders

Procedures:

  1. Identify six to eight key stakeholders for the issue and place their identifying name on each section of the smaller, inner wheel (e.g. parents, business leaders, youth, schools administrators, clergy).

  2. Divide group into the number of stakeholders named and have the group sit in a circle around the wheel.

  3. Each participant lines up with a stakeholder and places his/her name on a post-it on the larger wheel.

  4. Round one - Each participant must speak from the perspective of the aligned stakeholder.

  5. Round two - wheel turns - Each participant is now aligned with a new stakeholder and speaks from that point of view.

  6. Round three - and subsequent rounds - wheel turns again - Participants continue to speak from each new stakeholder's point of view.

  7. Continue dialogue until participants have spoken from every stakeholder perspective

  8. What did you learn? How did it feel to stand in other's shoes? What can be gained, individually and collectively, by taking the time to hear multiple perspectives?

[4]Adapted from Senge, P., Kleiner, A., Roberts, C., Ross, R. and Smith, B., *The Fifth Discipline Handbook*, Currency Doubleday, 1994.

Listening with a Third, Fourth and Fifth Ear[5]

Time: 30 minutes

Materials: Blindfolds: folded handkerchief or sport headband works well

Objective: To deepen dialogue through heightened attention to three levels of listening

Listening to Another = 'Third Ear'
Listening to Self = 'Fourth Ear'
Listening to Shared Meaning = 'Fifth Ear'

Attention to these (three) levels of listening invites participants to practise:

Inquiry (raising questions of others)
Advocacy (stating personal point of view)
Synthesis (summarising essence of group's conversation)

Procedures:

1. Provide general instructions about the role of three levels of listening in dialogue. Challenge each participant to practise inquiry, advocacy and synthesis as ways to deepen the dialogue through effective listening with their third, fourth and fifth ears.

2. Give each person a blindfold and explain that the blindfolds will be used to help heighten their attention to the three levels of listening. Encourage people to become comfortable with being blindfolded and, when they are ready, to begin a conversation with each other.

3. Allow the conversation to begin and move with its 'own life'. It may start out slowly due to the unfamiliar experience of being blindfolded. Let participants become comfortable with speaking to each other with blindfolds on. Eventually, the group will move past the awkwardness and into a deeper dialogue with one another, relying entirely on auditory cues instead of visual ones.

---

[5]Adapted form Elinor, L. and Girard, G., *Dialogue*, John Wiley and Sons, 1998, and Senge, P., Kleiner, A., Roberts, C., Ross, R. and Smith, B., *The Fifth Discipline Handbook*, Currency Doubleday, 1994.

---

4. Allow 10-15 minutes of engaged dialogue and respectfully close the activity with sensitivity to the ways in which blindfolds have heightened the experience of conversation.

5. Reflection: What did you notice?

Left-hand Column⁶

Time: 30-45 minutes

Materials: Sheet of lined paper and pen/pencil

Objective: To explore underlying beliefs, assumptions and judgments that usually go unspoken yet influence the quality of our dialogue with others

Procedures:

1. Recall a conversation you have had recently when you sensed frustration, anger, agitation or discomfort.

2. Context: Briefly write down a description of the issue: Who was involved and what happened?

3. Below this description: Draw a vertical line through the middle of the page to divide your paper into two columns.

4. Right-hand Column: In the right-hand column, carefully write a detailed 'script' of what you recall was said, naming each speaker followed by what was said in quotes.

5. Left-hand Column: Now go back and write in the *Left-hand Column* what you were really thinking and/or feeling during each 'line in the script', but did not say.

6. Reflection: What have you learnt? What would it take to be able to speak from the *Left-hand Column*? What would be a lasting outcome if we were able to reveal what was really going on?

7. Alternative Follow-up: After regular solo practice with *Left-hand Column* exercises and after significant trust has been built within a group - individuals and groups can be encouraged to share their *Left-hand Column* notes with others (first in pairs, then in small groups, and eventually with the full group).

---

⁶Adapted form Senge, P., Kleiner, A., Roberts, C., Ross, R. and Smith, B., *The Fifth Discipline Handbook*, Currency Doubleday, 1994.

How can we connect dialogue to action?

In his groundbreaking book *Strong Democracy* (1984), Benjamin Barber argues that there are nine functions of what he calls "strong democratic talk". His notion of strong democratic talk is very close to what we are calling the process of deepening the dialogue. These functions include:

1. The articulation of interests, bargaining and exchange
2. Persuasion
3. Agenda-setting
4. Exploring mutuality
5. Affiliation and affection
6. Maintaining autonomy
7. Witness and self-expression
8. Reformulation and reconceptualisation
9. Community-building as the creation of public interests, common goods and active citizens (pp.178-179).

One of the striking things about these functions is that they focus as much on the personal and affective as they do on the political and cognitive. They clearly give as much emphasis to the ways in which deep dialogue strengthens the bonds between people as to the new knowledge we gain when we gather with others for strong democratic talk. Barber goes on to say, however, that "all of the functions of talk discussed above converge toward a single, crucial end - the creation of a citizenry capable of genuinely public thinking and political judgment and thus able to envision a common future in terms of genuinely common goods" (p. 197).

Before that common future can be envisioned and acted upon, the hard work of deepening the dialogue must take place. When we engage in authentic, probing, reflective dialogue there is the potential to:

❖ bridge differences that have previously divided people
❖ transform how people see the world and one another
❖ build a new, healthier consensus
❖ discover new possibilities for cooperative action.

Authentic dialogue fuels every stage of community action. When it is consistently and painstakingly practised, it encourages public engagement and sustains community involvement and action. As Barber indicates, when time and energy are devoted to deepening the dialogue, community visioning is not only possible, it is the next necessary step. It is the bridge between talk and action, the link between authentic dialogue and meaningful work on behalf of the common good.

Perhaps the first step in connecting dialogue to action is to pose a series of questions:

What is our vision of an ideal community?

In what ways are we falling short of that ideal and which of our shortcomings cause us the greatest concern?

What is preventing us from addressing these concerns?

What first steps can we take? What issue or issues can we work on as a community to deal with these concerns?

Or more directly - What most needs to be done to positively change life in our community?

There is much to talk about here and the complexities of exploring such questions should not be underestimated. However, it is also certainly true that dialogue benefits from action, and community action is greatly spurred by dialogue. The sooner dialogue can lead to some kind of action, however modest, the more likely that the dialogue will be meaningfully sustained over time. We therefore recommend that teachers find a way to use their ongoing classroom conversations as an impetus for some kind of action in the school or community. The action may be as simple as joining together to clean up a park on a weekend, or visiting a home for elderly people. The point is to keep the conversation going in interesting and controversial directions but also to punctuate and animate the conversation with a series of actions that are consistent with the initial community visioning. The actions, whatever they are, must be occasions for further reflection and dialogue, not stand alone activities. Just as continuity is a desirable aspect of dialogue, so is it a necessary element of the ongoing interplay between talk and activity.

The beginnings of relating talk to action may be modest. However, the possibilities for engaging students in ambitious, community-wide projects are very real as long as the dialogue and action are meaningfully linked and both conversation and community service are sustained over time. We cannot emphasise enough the importance of keeping the discussion going and keeping the students engaged in some kind of ongoing work. When both are emphasised and given a prominent place in the school curriculum, much of the work of preparing students to be active members of a democratic society takes care of itself.

In other words, the best way to connect talk to action is to invite students to participate in continuous reflection. Whatever they are doing or talking about or studying, they should be encouraged to ask:

> What is happening?
> What have we observed?
> What have we learnt?
> How is it related to other things we have learnt?
> How might we do it differently next time?
> Why should we care?

By asking questions like these (our version of Deborah Meier's 'Habits of Mind'), students increase their understanding, sharpen their thinking and deepen their appreciation for the power of group deliberation. They begin to see that by talking together, acting together and reflecting together they can create a cooperative group of learners dedicated to making a decisive difference in the life of the larger community. Perhaps they will also come to acknowledge the wisdom of Margaret Mead's famous claim that the only thing that has ever made a difference in the world is small groups of people working together for change.

What thoughts would you like to add about connecting dialogue to action?

1.

2.

3.

Community Visioning

Time: Forty-five minutes to one hour

Materials: Coloured textas, two large pieces of butcher paper for each group, masking tape (hang drawings for group viewing and discussion)

Objective: To discover possibilities and opportunities for community action by drawing two 'views' of our community: (1) ideal vision and (2) what's real today

Procedures:

1. Divide each group into small work groups of four to six people.

2. Ask each group to work cooperatively together to create two drawings of our community:

    (1) Vision:
    Depict their desires and dreams for an ideal community.

    (2) Real:
    Show their 'real community' with images of obstacles and problems that stand in the way of reaching their vision, plus possible resources which might help overcome their concerns.

3. Have each group hang their community drawings side by side and describe both their ideal and real communities.

4. Reflection: What do you see? What are the possibilities? What are the obstacles? What community resources could be used to move from the present to the future vision? What is one significant action that could be taken, very realistically, from where we stand at the present? Who's willing to take it? What are the next steps?

Scarce and Changing Resources Collage

Time: At least one hour

Materials: Large stack of magazines, one set of textas, five glue sticks, five scissors, large butcher paper (one sheet/group)

Objective: To explore the dynamics of working together with scarce and changing resources

Procedures:

1. Divide into seven small groups through an arbitrary system that will create unbalanced numbers in each group (e.g. form groups with those who have the same shoes).

2. Explain the task and guidelines for being successful in completing the exercise

   Task: Complete a collage using pictures and no more than six hand-written words to capture your group's best thinking about optimum conditions for people working together in their community. Assign each group one of the eight following topics:

   1. Incentives and disincentives
   2. Power
   3. Skills and Knowledge
   4. Barriers
   5. Values
   6. Communication
   7. Resources
   8. Impact on People

   Guidelines: You are challenged to cooperate.
   'Every voice has a place at the table.'
   We only have limited resources (e.g. magazines, glue, scissors).

9. Give each group 20-30 minutes to work on their collage - announce time remaining at intervals.

10. Once groups have begun working well together, arbitrarily pick some people to form a new group for the remaining topic (the eighth topic has yet to be assigned). Also, arbitrarily move several people from established groups into a different group without explanation.

11. Call, 'Time is up'. Give each group two minutes to present their collage to the others.

12. Reflection:

    Note: This is a very meaty exercise and can be explored from many directions.

    What was hard, what was easy?

    How did you feel working as a group?

    How did different group sizes affect the work group's effectiveness?

    How were human resources used or ignored?

    What did work groups do to address the guidelines for success?

    How were needed resources (scissors, glue, magazines) distributed and shared, or kept just for some and not available for others?

    How did groups feel about having members moved to another group?

    How did the new group feel about a changed assignment?

    What did it feel like having new members join the group midway into the project?

    How were new members familiarised with what was already happening?

    What did the collages have to say about working together in communities?

    How does this exercise mirror what really happens in groups working on community projects?

    What can we learn from this exercise to bring more dialogue into action?

Post-It Planning Wall

Time: One hour

Materials: Large butcher paper, masking tape, square post-its, thin markers

Objective: To fully engage everyone in a visual, quick planning process that can also be
used to track and celebrate progress as things get done

Procedure:

1. Decide on a project.

2. Draw a picture (Community Visioning Activity) or capture key ideas about:

   Vision:
   What does this project look like when it is completed and successful?

   Reality:
   What barriers or obstacles do we face?

3. Decide Purpose: Why is this project important?

4. Set up a large time-line calendar. Make blocks for each day or week starting with
   today (beginning date) to when you want the project completed (ending date).

5. Brainstorm all the tasks that need to be done. Write each task with an action verb
   on one post-it. For example, a community clean-up project might have tasks like
   making posters and flyers, distributing posters and flyers to schools and community
   businesses, purchasing garbage bags, recruiting volunteers from neighbouring
   schools, typing volunteer sign-up sheets, purchasing drinks for work day, getting
   donated food for celebration.

6. Review each post-it and assign to a person who will be responsible for getting it
   done. Write the name in the top left hand corner.

7. Block out the time and sequence of tasks that need to be done by placing the
   post-its on the calendar and assign each a deadline. Write the date in the top
   right-hand corner.

8. Review the planning post-its and fill in any missing tasks that now come to mind - write a post-it for each additional task and place on the planning calendar. If, again, the project is community cleanup, additional tasks might include asking neighbourhood schools to announce the project during 'morning messages'. One might want to call the local newspaper for an interview, etc.

9. Review progress, as a group, on a regular basis. Cross out each accomplished task with a bold red line across the post-it. Move post-it to new date if behind schedule.

10. Celebrate every small task (a red line) when it gets done!

11. Celebrate the overall success of the project when it is completed!

Community Evaluation

Time: One hour

Materials: Flip chart and textas

Objective: To involve everyone who has worked on a community project to evaluate its success and learn ways to improve how they work together for the next project

Procedures:

1. After celebrating the completion of a project, take time to evaluate what has been learnt through working together.

2. On a big flip chart, draw a vertical line down the centre and label the left side 'What Worked' and label the right side 'What Didn't Work' (or could be improved).

3. Brainstorm and list specific things that the group observed worked, did not work, or might have worked better.

   Note: You can also go through categories for specific activities that were relevant to the project (e.g. planning, fund-raising, publicity, recruitment of volunteers)

4. Reflection - After a thorough list has been made, ask the group:

   What have we learnt?
   What would we like to do differently next time?

Conclusion

In conclusion, we affirm that civic renewal is impossible without passionate, engaging dialogue. The complex challenges of community life in this century require solutions that can and must emerge from earnest collaboration through determined dialogue. Dialogue unleashes creative possibilities for our schools as well as our communities, transforming us as individuals, while increasing our collective understanding and emboldening our collective will. Our capacity to learn from each other through democratic discourse despite major differences in experience and viewpoint can lead directly to decisive civic action that promotes social justice and mutual respect.

It is imperative, however, that schools take the lead in using dialogue to prepare our next generation of citizens and community leaders. We are convinced that when thoughtful discussion is firmly rooted in our classrooms, educational transformation can occur. Such a transformation may begin with students - but it will also affect teachers, administrators, families and the whole community. School reform efforts that include the potent practice of dialogue create possibilities for authentic change from the 'inside-out'.

Just imagine what can happen when classrooms become places where students are encouraged to passionately exchange their most deeply held convictions about the issues that matter to them most. Or picture how much more enthusiastic teachers and administrators will be regarding their work when they are regularly engaged in discussions that help them to think through solutions for improving their school. Or consider how much more vital and energetic our schools and communities will be when citizens are invited to participate in conversations that encourage them to raise concerns and to collaborate on what needs to be done to make their schools and communities better.

Making dialogue an essential part of teaching and learning is likely to have a much greater long-term impact than policy mandates imposed from the 'outside-in' or from the 'top-down'. Dialogue can facilitate reform that happens from the 'inside-out', beginning with students and their teachers, extending to administrators and parents, and proceeding to the community at large. Democratic participation through dialogue challenges each of us to re-imagine the possibilities for a more cooperative and harmonious society and to begin the work, both individually and collectively, that will help to make such a society a reality.

Finally, it is our contention that the practice of dialogue is entirely consistent with a variety of proposals that have been put forward to reform schools. One of the most prominent and impressive of these proposals is advanced by the American reformer and researcher Linda Darling-Hammond (1997). At the heart of her proposal are nine conditions that she believes are associated with meaningful student learning.

How Dialogue Supports Darling-Hammond's Nine Conditions for Meaningful Student Learning[7]

1. **Active In-Depth Learning**

    Such learning begins with a serious and profound exploration of the disciplines in which teachers employ 'higher-order thinking, consideration of alternatives, use of core ideas and modes of inquiry in a discipline, extended writing, and an audience beyond the school for student work'. Virtually all of these require students to develop skill at articulating and defending ideas and at listening closely and discerningly to what others have to say. The skills of speaking, listening, thinking and collaborating - the heart of dialogue - are undoubtedly one of the chief spurs to active in-depth learning.

2. **Emphasis on Authentic Performance**

    Assessments that have real-world value are increasingly emphasised in school. One aspect of those assessments that emerges repeatedly is the ability to present ideas clearly and cogently. As researcher Ann Brown has pointed out, the members of an audience witnessing an authentic assessment expect coherence, good explanations, and clarification of obscure points. One of the best ways to practise and hone these skills is through dialogue.

3. **Attention to Development**

    As Darling-Hammond observes, development of all kinds - cognitive, physical, social, emotional and moral - is greatly enhanced by the quality of educational experiences students enjoy. We know, particularly through the work of Lawrence Kohlberg on moral development, that when learners at different levels of development come together to dialogue, those at lower levels are stretched to new plateaus of understanding and sensitivity. Dialogue, particularly dialogue that stresses collaboration and cooperation, is an ideal forum for educating and supporting heterogeneous groups of students. Citing Vygotsky to reinforce further the developmental benefits of dialogue, Darling-Hammond writes that "when children use language they are not only verbalising their internal thinking processes but also aiding their conceptual development".

---

[7]From Darling-Hammond, L., *The Right to Learn*, Jossey-Bass, (1997)

---

4. Appreciation for Diversity

It almost goes without saying that dialogue can contribute greatly to enhancing appreciation for diversity. When people from diverse backgrounds gather to share experiences, perspectives and ideas and do so in a setting in which close listening and mutual respect are assiduously practised, diversity tends to be embraced as a valuable group strength. As Paulo Freire has noted, ongoing dialogue not only increases appreciation for diversity, it also builds a strong sense of "unity within diversity".

5. Opportunities for Collaborative Learning

Darling-Hammond says that "learning-centred classrooms feature student talk and collective action". Learning in the real world is largely social, and there is simply no better way to foster social learning than through dialogue. Or as Darling-Hammond puts it, with great simplicity: "Talking is a vehicle for learning". She also quotes Deborah Meier to the effect that good "teaching is mostly listening and learning is mostly telling". The link between dialogue and the development of learning of all kinds - especially collaborative learning - is indisputable.

6. A Collective Perspective Across the School

The best schools are steeped in shared norms that are built up over time. One of the best ways to create such norms and to sustain them is through classroom discussions. Thinking through and deciding together what the students and teachers in a school most value and are most committed to, depends in large part on carving out class time to talk, argue, and reach new mutual understanding about what the school should stand for.

7. Structures for Caring

Relationships matter, sustaining people through adversity matters, building self-esteem matters, showing people on a regular basis that you care deeply about their welfare matters. All of these structures for caring are supported and enhanced by the practice of respectful and appreciative dialogue.

8. Support for Democratic Learning

Perhaps the most obvious connection between the practice of dialogue and creating conditions for learning and understanding is in the area of fostering democratic learning. Dialogue gives students a voice in creating a more powerful learning environment and teaches them how to advocate for issues that they feel strongly about. If part of the function of education is to prepare students for participation in a democratic society, there is no better way to carry out this function than to give students some say through dialogue and mutual persuasion in what they will learn and how they will learn it.

9. **Connections to Family and Community**

   Such connections can be greatly strengthened through well-defined structures for ongoing communication. Students should be encouraged to play a role in sustaining such structures for communication in both informal and formal ways. Informally, students can dialogue with parents regularly about what they are learning and what they need to learn more effectively and thoroughly. Formally, students can periodically communicate with the community through a variety of means - some of which should take the form of discussion forums and study groups in which dialogue is highly prized.

Whether it is promoting active, in-depth learning, appreciating diversity, encouraging collaboration, or supporting democratic learning, dialogue has an important - even decisive role to play in making our schools better and our communities more involved. We end where we began - affirming our belief in the rich and stimulating possibilities that dialogue affords, and celebrating the joys and delights that good conversation engenders. Dialogue not only helps us to learn from one another and to appreciate one another more fully, it is also one of the things that gives our lives meaning and satisfaction. Without dialogue, our lives are greatly diminished. With it, our lives are immeasurably enriched.

Appendix

What follows is a case study of the ins and outs of making dialogue work in classroom settings. A textbook or manual may give the impression that teaching effectively is simply a matter of following the steps provided. Yet, we all know that good teaching is itself a dialogue between teacher, students and subject.

Debbie Trujillo, who worked with us in one of the workshops we presented, decided to use the framework of the six guiding questions to inform her teaching in year seven reading at Belen Middle School. The first narrative describes her experiences as she tried to introduce dialogue to her students. After using the activities from this manual, dialogue became an essential part of her teaching and learning practices with her year seven students.

On a day that George Otero observed her class, near the end of the school year, students were well organised for engaging dialogue. They walked excitedly into the class, picked up the question sheet on school safety (see a copy of this sheet at the conclusion of the appendix), identified a group discussion leader, passed out talking sticks, and initiated the discussion. All of this occurred with little help from Debbie. In fact, she did not participate in the discussion at all. At this advanced stage in their development as discussants, students gave little thought to the earning or losing of points (one of the original motivators for participating in discussion as Debbie's story indicates) and assessment was no longer the issue. Students wanted to talk and listen to each other. They looked forward to discussing school safety with each other. The discussion itself had become its own reward.

As you can see from the questions that students discussed, the processes of circular response, active listening, and open, public discussion build critical thinking very effectively.

We enclose the full list of discussion questions because we know that school safety is an issue that most students are eager to explore.

Debbie Trujillo
Belen Middle School
Year Seven Reading

Since our first meeting, I have used the circle discussion several times in my classroom.

The circle discussion has been wonderful. I have never been able to conduct any kind of organised discussion in my classroom. Everyone shared but nobody would listen. After the workshop, I explained the circle discussion to several of my classes and had them practise.

The 'practice' didn't go well. The same students who always spoke up were willing to share and the quiet students remained quiet. I shared this with a teacher from the high school. She told me she attached a mark to the activities. So that's what I did.

I have a supply of different coloured icy-pole sticks. I give each student three sticks of the same colour and students sitting next to each other get different colours. This ensures that nobody 'passes' a stick to her or his neighbour. When we do the circle discussion students pass a stick to the facilitator each time they share. If more than one student has a hand raised, the facilitator calls on the person with the most sticks remaining. This helps give all the students an equal opportunity to express an opinion.

At the end of the discussion, I assign marks according to how many sticks each student has left in his/her possession. Zero sticks = 100%, one stick = 90%, two sticks = 80%, three sticks = 70%. Also, while the discussion is taking place, the facilitator takes note of anyone who interrupts, speaks out of turn or holds a private conversation with a neighbour. Each incident equals five points off their mark.

This worked great! The students listened to one another, the number of students who still chose not to express an opinion in any way has been drastically reduced and the kids love circle discussion.

I initially used circle discussion as a pre-reading activity for a novel we were about to begin. The issues in the novel include death, organ transplant, prejudice, poverty, family, love and friendship. I typed up statements pertaining to organ transplants that included controversial ideas about several of the issues.

Since then, we used circle discussion to talk about the novel and issues as they came up.

I was pleased with circle discussion and thought it went very well, but I also wanted to get feedback from the students. I asked them to write a paragraph explaining their likes and dislikes about circle discussion. Below are some of their statements about why they liked it:

"…you can learn stuff."

"I like to hear other people's opinions. I also like to say my opinions. I think we learn more in circle discussion."

"I like how everybody says something different about the same subject."

"It is kind of fun that we can all say what we feel."

"…because we can discuss what we like and what we don't like."

"…you get to talk and listen."

"…helps us get over being scared to talk in front of the class and speak freely without any problems."

"…because everyone has to be part of it."

"…you can see everyone."

"…teaches you how to listen and how to express your opinion out loud."

"I think this could be useful for primary kids because it can teach them to speak up and not to be afraid of speaking their minds. It can also teach how to listen."

"…teaches you to be quiet."

"It is a good way to develop patience."

"…we cooperate more with one another."

"…it helps you listen to people and people pay attention to you and it helps you get along with other people."

"…you get to hear everyone's opinion, then that opens your mind a little more."

"I think it's a better way to communicate."

"…good way to express yourself."

"When we get icy-pole sticks it helps us talk because we have to get rid of them."

"…involves a lot of communication and teamwork."

"…express our feelings about whatever without being interrupted."

"…is a very nice socialising activity."

"…cool hearing what other people think."

"…really saying what we want."

"…helps my listening skills."

"…learnt a great deal about our topic and other people."

There was only one negative comment. "It can get boring if you're on one topic too long and the topic is boring."

The other change I made to the circle discussion is that I appointed a student to be the facilitator. The discussion proceeds just as smoothly and the students follow the guidelines just as if I was facilitating.

School Safety Discussion Questions

What was your reaction to the Columbine High School shootings?

In your opinion, what can teachers, administration, etc. do to prevent tragedies like the shooting at Columbine High School? What can we do to increase school safety at Belen Middle School?

In your opinion, what can you, the individual student, do to prevent tragedies and increase school safety at Belen Middle School?

Do you think our school is safe? Why or why not? What do you think needs improvement? What can we do to improve?

Do you believe having teachers on duty before and after school helps our school be a safe place? How about the security guard? The police officers who are here these three weeks? How do you feel having police officers on campus? Do you think it's a good idea?

If you were superintendent of Belen schools, what specific things would you do to improve Belen Middle School and, more specifically, make BMS safe?

The boys who did the shooting at Columbine High School were somewhat 'out' or not part of the 'main crowd'. Some people think this contributed to their motive for what they did? Do you agree or disagree?

Acceptance is very important for all human beings. What can each of you do to help students who aren't very popular, who don't have many/any friends, or are 'different' from the 'main crowd'?

Do you think the media (television, newspapers, magazines) help the general public by reporting the news and/or happenings at a tragedy such as the one that occurred at Columbine or do you think they made the problem worse by giving it so much attention that it encourages other psycho/crazy people to do 'copycat' crimes?

Would you like to see such devices as metal detectors installed here at your schools?

Sometimes people are judged by what they wear. Do you believe school uniforms would help increase school safety?

Barber, B. (1984). *Strong Democracy*. Berkeley: University of California Press.

Bohm, D. (1996). *On Dialogue*. London: Routledge.

Bridges, D. (1988). *Education, Democracy, and Discussion*. Lanham Md: University Press of America.

Brookfield, S. and Preskill, S. (1999). *Discussion as a Way of Teaching*. San Francisco: Jossey-Bass.

Bruffee, K. (1993). *Collaborative Learning*. Baltimore: Johns Hopkins University Press.

Burbules, N. (1993). *Dialogue in Teaching*. New York: Teachers College Press

Darling-Hammond, L. (1997). *The Right to Learn*. San Francisco: Jossey-Bass.

Dewey, J. (1916). *Democracy and Education*. Old Tappan, NJ: Macmillan.

Elinor, L. and Girard, G. (1998). *Dialogue*. New York: John Wiley and Sons.

Freire, P. (1994). *Pedagogy of Hope*. New York: Continuum.

Gastil, J. (1993). *Democracy in Small Groups*. Philadelphia: New Society Publishers.

Grudin, R. (1996). *On Dialogue*. Boston: Houghton Mifflin.

Meier, D. (1995). *The Power of Their Ideas*. Boston: Beacon Press National Issues Forums. Dayton, Ohio: Kettering Foundation.

Palmer, P. (1993). *To Know as We are Known*. San Francisco: Harper San Francisco.

Resnick, L. (1987). 'Learning In School and Out.' <u>Educational Researcher.</u>

Senge, P., Kleiner, A., Roberts, C., Ross, R. and Smith, B. (1994). *The Fifth Discipline Handbook*. New York: Currency Doubleday.

Wood, G. (1992). *Schools That Work*. New York: Dutton.

About the Authors

George Otero, Ed.D:

Founder and director of Las Palomas de Taos, a nonprofit educational centre devoted to innovative programs and workshops that increase people's understanding of the world as well as the art, culture and history of the Southwest. Pioneer in the field of confronting global and multicultural issues by bringing together diverse groups to meet challenges of a changing world. More than 25 years experience in wide range of educational disciplines, having taught all ages (children to adults) and worked with foundations, international educational organisations, churches, businesses, public and private schools and state agencies. Co-developed and instituted Global Realities and Youth Leadership Challenge, a national youth leadership program. Directed national teacher centre at University of Denver. Has presented at over 500 workshops, conferences and retreats nationally. Has developed curriculum and published book/journal articles on global and multicultural education. Has served as instructor, trainer, consultant, keynote speaker, grant writer and curriculum developer at the University of Denver, University of Northern Colorado and Metropolitan State College in Denver. Board member, New Mexico Community Education Association.

Lois W. Vermilya

Twenty-two years community education experience with diverse tribes and communities in United States and Latin America. Provided 17 years of executive leadership to Futures for Children, an international nonprofit organisation promoting shared leadership, collaboration, change management and diversified funding. Developed community-based initiatives; youth leadership training; intergenerational educational strategies; and community-wide training in deliberation, facilitation and community action. Has organised national conferences and international education convenings, integrating culturally diverse and cross-generation participation. Invited presenter and facilitator to various national meetings. Author and editor for resource publications for community education and leadership development. Independent consulting contracts for Puente Project, the Getty Information Institute; the New Mexico Centre for Dispute Resolution; The Hitachi Foundation; UNM Office of Contract Archeology in coordination with All Indian Pueblo Council, among others. Cultural and Symbolic Anthropologist: BA summa cum laude, Colgate University; MA, University of New Mexico; Phi Beta Kappa.

Stephen Preskill, PhD:

Associate Professor of Education in the Division of Educational Leadership and Organisational Learning at the University of New Mexico. Fifteen years of experience in higher education in addition to nine years of teaching in public schools. Has written widely for professional journals about educational reform, biographies of educational leaders, promoting democracy through dialogue, and narratives of exemplary teaching. Coauthor of a 1999 book for Jossey-Bass entitled *Discussion as a Way of Teaching: Tools and Techniques for Democratic Classrooms*. Also completing a coauthored book for Prentice Hall focusing on teachers' stories. BA in History from Ithaca College; MA in History and Education from Long Island University; Med in Special Education from the University of Vermont; PhD in Educational Policy Studies from University of Illinois at Urbana.

Workshops, Presentations and Trainings

Dr George Otero and Associates are available to conduct a number of specialised trainings, workshops, seminars and conference presentations throughout Australia in the following areas:

Middle Years of Schooling

Student Engagement

The Global Classroom - Curriculum for the 21st Century

Student Leadership Conferences and Workshops

Teacher PD

RelationaLearning™ - A new model of teaching and learning

Skills for Democracy - Teaching dialogue in the classroom

Community-Based Curriculum

For more information on how you can obtain publications and/or schedule a training event or program with Dr George Otero and Associates, contact the publisher:

Hawker Brownlow Education
P.O. Box 580
Cheltenham Vic 3192
Phone: (03) 9555 1344
Fax: (03) 9553 4538
Website: http://www.hbe.com.au
Email: brown@hbe.com.au

or contact Dr George Otero directly at:

1918 Fort Union Drive
Santa Fe, New Mexico 87505
United States of America
Phone: 0011 505 988 9556
Fax: 0011 505 986 0339
Email: sunmoon@newmexico.com